Humility

by Dom André Louf

*All booklets are published thanks to the
generous support of the members of the
Catholic Truth Society*

CATHOLIC TRUTH SOCIETY
PUBLISHERS TO THE HOLY SEE

Contents

———⊰⊱———

———⊰⊱———

1. Humility

An ancient story relates how one day, as St Anthony of Eygpt[1] was going out of his hermitage, he saw all the devil's temptations thrown like an immense net over the earth. He moaned with fright and exclaimed: "My God, who then can be saved?" And a voice answered from heaven: "Humility". Another story of St Anthony's goes like this: "Suppress all temptation, and no-one will be saved". The conclusion is obvious: in the Christian life, however inevitable temptations are, so too is the practice of humility inescapable.

"Humility in the monastic life", such was the theme proposed for this book. I say proposed, but it was imposed, with such gentle and friendly

---

[1] See page 41 for short biographies of Church Fathers mentioned in the text.

pressure that I could not resist it. Very early on, however, I found myself in a state of deep embarrassment. Who was I to speak of humility? Was I giving the impression that I am an expert, or even an example, on the subject? How is it possible to pretend to be such a thing without by the same token proving just the opposite? "To believe that one is not proud is one of the clearest manifestations that one actually is", said St John Climacus. And to believe that one is humble is a worse illusion still. It is even ridiculous.

There is one more snare here also: the mention of the monastic life, as the place of our enquiries. Is humility then the prerogative of monks? Are they more advanced in humility than other Christians? Far from it! And I would even say: no, on the contrary! Their very vocation to the monastic life exposes them more than other Christians to the failing of thinking themselves better than others.

In some amusing pages whose fine psychological analyses have not been bettered, St John Cassian describes this ultimate and perfidious trick of the devil who succeeds, even with great ascetics, in turning the greatest exploits of asceticism to vainglory. The spirit of vainglory thus subtly trips up the monk - this is the image he uses - through self-esteem, whose last refuge is false humility. And Cassian completes his statement with a few examples sketched from life: "The monk who remained unmoved by subtle flattery is crushed through the vainglory conferred by the prestige of his silence. Should he fast publicly, he is tempted to glorify himself for it; but if he hides it for fear of any glory he could obtain from it, he still falls into vainglory. If, to avoid this, he avoids making long prayers in the presence of his brethren, he does not escape the sting of vanity precisely because he is hiding in order to pray, and no-one can see him..." And Cassian goes on: "This evil does not seek to harm the monk by any means other than his own virtues". One can already guess the extreme difficulty there is in discerning between true and false humility.

Speaking of humility is not easy for other reasons too, particularly nowadays. All our great "masters of suspicion", or almost all, have wanted to attack it. For Nietzsche, humility is the great lie of the weak, who thus transform their cowardice into an apparent virtue. For Freud, it is a masochistic variant of the guilt complex. For Adler, it is close to a simple feeling of inferiority. Their interpretations have left their mark on our modern culture. How can humility be reconciled with the famous "assertiveness" which is so extolled by psychologists from across the Atlantic, and with some reason too? How is it possible to honour the last place preached by the Gospel, in a society which is only impressed by the success of "young Turks" in politics, or "golden boys" in economics?

11. Is Humility a Virtue?

———◆———

I would also like to draw attention to another problem, which is much less visible but all the more insidious and which, it seems to me, is responsible in a large part for the difficulty there is nowadays in speaking of Christian humility. This problem has been felt throughout the history of spirituality, and remains unconsciously in many minds. It expresses itself through an ambiguity which is attached to the notion of humility. On the one hand, following Scripture and Tradition, spiritual authors have given it an eminent position in spiritual experience. On the other hand, when they try to describe Christian virtue as a coherent whole, they find it difficult to find a logical position that would explain this priority, though everyone is convinced of its importance, as Anthony's story, quoted above, already illustrates.

A more precise analysis of the causes of this problem would exceed the object of this book. But at least we may say this. In the eyes of the Gospel and of the spiritual masters, it seems that the ambiguity lies in the very notion of *virtue*. The concept as well as the word - *aretē* - (roughly equivalent to excellence in Greek) are not found among the words of Jesus or in the Gospel. The two letters of Peter mention it three times, but in two of these occurrences, the word is attributed to God and is a synonym of "glory of God" (*1 Peter* 2, 3; *2 Peter* 1, 3). In the third case, it appears among a series of qualities recognised in the believer, and surrounded by faith and knowledge (*2 Peter* 1, 5).

Saint Paul only uses it once, in passing, in Philippians 4, 8. Virtue-*aretē* is here once again placed among other Christian qualities, and in this case is synonymous with "good renown". Paul does not think at all of the concept of virtue, which was at that time a term used by Greek philosophers. The Syriac translation of this passage, which may perhaps go right back to an ancient version in Aramaic, may give a better interpretation. It translates it as "works of glory and praise", works that in the context of his letter, Paul wishes on his correspondents, so that their way of living may be known and appreciated by their contemporaries.

This difficulty about humility seen as a virtue is reflected in patristic literature, and right up until the Middle Ages. On one hand, they unanimously attribute humility an important place, which is in fact absolutely unavoidable for spiritual progress. For Augustine, for example, it summarises all Christian discipline: "*Humilitas pene una disciplina christiana est*" "Humility is the only thing required for the Christian life". For Cassian, it is "the mother and mistress of every virtue", and he adds an important point in relating it to pagan virtues: "It is the proper and magnificent gift of the Saviour". And we could multiply the number of quotations.

But on the other hand, the same patristic tradition feels some difficulty in expressing this absolute primacy of humility among the categories of moral philosophy that it has to use when seeking to define Christian ethics. We find ourselves here in the presence of a typical case of faith inculturation in an environment which is not adapted to it. It is a very instructive case too. Such inculturation is absolutely necessary, and even inescapable since it would take place anyway without us, and in that case against us, but it always carries some risk. Indeed, the experience of faith is then threatened with being somewhat twisted or even deformed in one direction or the other, according to the particular mind-set of the environment in which it becomes embodied. And so, in the case of humility, we have the right to ask ourselves if, during the process of inculturation, it may have become a victim of some fatal deviations.

This risk obviously increases as the theoretician of humility speaks without any real experience of it. "Christianity then risks" - noted Pseudo-Makarius - "letting itself be carried outside its limits, and ends up having the same meaning as atheism". High stakes indeed! For these realities, he adds, "come to pass mysteriously in our hearts, through the work of the Holy Spirit, and it is only then that we may speak of them".

But has a "pagan" humility ever existed? The leading lights of the great patristic period could not avoid the question, particularly as most of them sought to discover among the best thinkers of Antiquity some presentiment of Christian realities which in them would have already been a fruit of grace. However, they are divided on the subject. The Greek Fathers were rather favourable to their brothers in the Greek culture. Clement of Alexandria, for example, thinks he has found humility mentioned in one of Plato's texts. Origen, commenting on the *Magnificat* and the Virgin's humility, explains that ancient philosophers knew it under the name of *metriotēs*, or measure, moderation, *mediocritas*. Thus he opened a dangerous way, full of pitfalls, on which Saint Thomas Aquinas and then a whole section of spiritual writings would happily follow suit.

Saint Augustine seems to have been the first to strongly affirm the exclusive Christian character of humility, and so to maintain that pagan authors could not have known it, whether they were Epicureans, Stoics or Platonists. Even the best among them did not know humility, he claims, since "it comes from elsewhere, from the One who, being the Most High, wished to humble himself for us". What the Bishop of Hippo expresses here as a theoretician of spirituality only repeats what many spiritual people, following Anthony's story quoted at the start, had already lived and expressed in their own way.

But the notion of a humility acceptable in the eyes of ancient philosophy did not die easily and lasted much longer. And we may ask ourselves if it does not survive, in a more or less rampant way, in the subconscious of our time's Christian culture. It is possible that Saint Thomas Aquinas may be held responsible in some way for this slight drift. As I have just mentioned, the Angelic Doctor, at first somewhat embarrassed not to have found humility listed among the virtues by Aristotle, made his own Origen's opinion, who understood it under the platonic concept of *metriotēs*; in this case it would be understood as moderation, measure or temperance. Indeed it is, if we may say so, as a sort of by-product of the virtue of temperance that Saint Thomas would catalogue Christian humility. He explains his choice: it is a repressive virtue, says he, since its role is to repress the appetites and desires which, without it, would be tempted to use all their desiring energy *praeter rationem*, contrary to right reason. Aristotle is then invoked, as well as Cicero in whom Saint Thomas finds humility under the virtue of modesty.

Saint Thomas's task was a delicate one. He was careful to keep a right balance within the catalogue of philosophical virtues, between one virtue and its opposite, thus opening the way for a virtuous *mediocritas: in medio stat virtus* (virtue stands in the middle). Now, in Aristotle's perspective, the opposite of moderation is magnanimity, or courage, which should not be imperilled by an excess of self-depreciation. Saint Thomas, who had learned this well, engaged in touching dialectical contortions to save both humility, which the Greeks have in fact superbly ignored, and magnanimity in both its lay and Christian meaning.

Let us not throw stones at Saint Thomas, who had the immense merit of starting a largely successful process of inculturation of the Gospel in Aristotelian thought. However, one is entitled to ask if, in such a system, humility is not rather straightened, or even out of place, in relation to the central role that it plays in Christian experience.

Moreover, several times, in passages which I will not pursue here, Saint Thomas, perhaps aware of a deviation in his thinking, tried to restore the balance in favour of humility. But not all the Christian Aristotelians of the late Middle Ages followed him. For example, dazzled by the beautiful edifice of the philosophical virtues, Siger of Brabant, an Aristotelian of the strictest observance, pushed to the limit the reticence of ancient thought. For him, "magnanimity is a more perfect virtue than humility", the latter being the virtue of the "less perfect", of the mediocre in other words, while magnanimity is the prerogative of the strong! These are almost Nietzschean tones! But why reply this way? One could simply object as follows; "And on the cross, was Jesus magnanimous or humble?".

The reaction was not slow to come. It came from a Franciscan theologian. For Saint Francis asserted that poverty and humility were two sisters, and he wanted them to be practiced equally by his disciples, to whom he gave the beautiful name of *fratres minores* (literally "low brothers", better known as friars minor). So it was the Franciscan Saint Bonaventure who reacted forcefully. In his eyes, it would be perfectly vain to look for Christian humility in Aristotle, or to explain it from reason alone. It can only be understood from within faith in Jesus Christ. And, he added, let us stop going on about a so-called magnanimity that would be threatened by humility. For him, the real magnanimity is humility!

This brief overview of the conflicts surrounding the concept of humility suffices to clarify its position which is paradoxical or even precarious - and in this sense, fully evangelical. If the theologians of the spiritual life experience some hesitation in classifying it correctly within a catalogue of virtues whose origins remain pagan, such is not the case with those whose knowledge is based on experience. We have already heard a few say something on the subject, but one could make a whole list of passages that witness to its exceptional importance. Two final examples should convince us: one Mother of the Desert - (for there were authentic Mothers of the Desert at the same time as the Fathers) -, who was called Theodora, affirms this without hesitation: "It is not ascetic practice, nor vigils, nor any other work that can save us but only sincere humility". Isaac the Syrian interchanged the terms of that statement, and thus makes it even more peremptory: "Even without works, humility obtains forgiveness..., but without it, works profit us nothing... What salt is to food, humility is to the virtues, but without it, all our works are in vain, as are every virtue and ascetic practice." Isaac says it well: the salt of the virtues. For, if we absolutely insist on recognising it as a virtue, still it must be quite a different sort of virtue. Saint Basil, who maintains this expression used in philosophy, calls it *panaretos*, the "most virtuous one", what we may call the all-encompassing one, since it contains all the others.

———◆———

III. Humility: Life Experience

―――――――

*B*ut if one were to define humility at all cost as a virtue or more particularly as the standard by which one measures one's self-esteem, the very meaning of humility would become diluted. So, in the second part of this discussion, I would like to present humility to you as a concrete experience related to a particular, evangelical situation, an experience lived by the first monks and described as an essential stage in any Christian experience. We will ask ourselves what is happening in this concrete experience, and we will try to indicate how to live it.

It will not therefore be about the virtue of humility, but rather about a state of humility, that is, in the original meaning of the Greek work *tapeinôsis*, a state of abasement, or from the Latin *humilitas*, (*humus* which means earth or soil), a state where one finds oneself literally at ground level. It is a state which is absolutely indispensable for a virtue to be born from it. Already Saint Bernard had noted: *"Sin humiliatione, nulla humilitas"*, without a concrete abasement, there is no humility.

I do not intend here to make a detailed study of the Christological root of this state of abasement but it is self-evident that this is where it comes now. Saint Paul has shed light on it magnificently in his hymn of the Letter to the Philippians, with its double movement of descent and of elevation: "He humbled himself and therefore he has been exalted" (*Philippians* 2). This double movement must have been offered to the disciples more than once by Jesus, since we find this *"logion"* (saying) mentioned in many places in the synoptic gospels, and elsewhere in the New Testament: "Whoever exalts himself will be humbled". (*Matthew* 23:12; *Luke* 14:11; 18:14). And whoever has refused to do the same, God himself undertakes to make him undergo this experience: "And you, Capernaum, will you be exalted to heaven? You shall be brought down to Hades" (*Luke* 10:15), into that "hell" which at that moment was in the mind of Jesus, the place that he would soon visit in his death, in order to triumph over it.

When we talk about the humility of Jesus, we are not speaking of some quality which he came down to give us an example of, but on the contrary we must see it as a true saving way, whose first stage consists in an inevitable abasement. It is the paschal journey, which every Christian is invited to travel with Jesus. For Jesus, this journey included a confrontation with the Prince of evil, from the first temptations in the desert until their culminating point in the garden of Gethsemane, the Passion and on the cross. For the disciples, the way will also be marked out by temptation, which is both unavoidable and the only way to salvation. This is the deeper meaning of Saint Anthony's dictum already quoted above: "Suppress all temptation, and no-one will be saved". To want to avoid it would be useless, and sooner or later we would still be obliged to undergo it. There is no escape, either for the monk in the desert or for the Christian in the world, since both the desert and the world are places of temptation. The only difference between the two is that the monk, led by the Spirit, goes out willingly to meet temptation.

As for what happens at the heart of temptation, Jesus described it for the use of his apostles, in a short sentence pronounced at the moment where he himself, sorrowful even unto death, was prey to his decisive temptation: "Watch and pray that you may not enter into temptation; the spirit indeed is willing, but the flesh is weak."(*Matthew* 26:41). Two opposite forces confront each other, fighting for the hearts of Jesus and of his disciples: the flesh, infirm and weak, and the spirit, willing of course, but terribly hindered by the impulses of the flesh. Jesus counsels a double attitude: watching and praying. For it is in the midst of temptation, more than anywhere else, that the believer, already shaken by the flesh's complicity, feels the absolute necessity of God's help: and he asks for it. It is there, at the heart of the crisis that, like a gift from the Spirit, true humility will begin and will enable them to undergo temptation with a minimum of risk.

This battle between flesh and spirit, between sin and grace, between man and the Spirit of God, therefore implies a double consciousness: that of the abyss of weakness that characterises the potential sinners that we are at that moment, and that of the gentle and delicate, but finally irresistible strength of grace. No-one has described the redoubtable risks of this process better than Saint John Cassian. When temptation becomes so insistent that it risks overwhelming everything in its fall. With the awareness of weakness comes another awareness that helps maintain its balance. It is while he is prey to temptation that man perceives the action of grace within himself. This action operates in the very midst of the moans that the brutality of the assault draws from him, and nourishes his prayer which now becomes constant.

"Let us learn also, then", writes Cassian, "to feel in each action both our weakness and the help of God, and to proclaim daily with the saints: 'I was pushed hard, so I was falling, but the Lord helped me. The Lord is my strength and my song; he has become my salvation.'" (*Psalm* 118:13-14).

We must see "both our weakness and God's help", said Cassian. A text by Isaac the Syrian, recently discovered but not yet published in the Syriac original, describes with a different vocabulary this same strange coalition between sin and grace. Isaac exhorts the hermit to watch carefully in his heart for the succession of consolations and temptations that occur there. This is how he will learn to know both his weakness and the strength of grace. He says: "the hermits who watch themselves in every battle of their asceticism, see this strength spiritually..., they perceive when it withdraws and when it comes near. They take note of the change that occurs in them, emanating both from this indescribable strength that suddenly surges in them, and from their natural weakness. Many times, this strength changes the body at the same time as the spirit. May the one who has experienced this understand! Brethren, it is advisable to reflect carefully on this. Thanks to this continual observation (what happens at the moment of temptation), the one who learns from it acquires an infinitely great humility, as well as an unshakeable faith in God".

What then is man's role in this battle going on at the heart of temptation? It reduces itself, explains Cassian, "*ut quotidie astrahentem nos gratiam Dei humiliter subsequamur*", to follow step by step, humbly and every day, the grace of God who is attracting us. And he clarifies later the meaning of the adverb "humbly", by linking it to David's repentance: "*quod peccatum suum humiliatus agnoscit, suum est*". David's part was to recognise his sin, after being humiliated; God's part was then to grant forgiveness. "After having been humiliated by his weakness", after having crossed the fire of temptation or even, as in David's case, the bitter defeat of sin. We must not worry if that was the only means left to God to make us realise both our weakness and his grace. An ancient saying had already insinuated this: "I prefer a defeat humbly borne to a victory obtained by pride". Saint Bernard said the same thing: "To a proud virgin God prefers a repented sinner".

IV. The Broken Heart

We find ourselves at the heart of the process from which humility some day will be born. Helplessness is at its centre. To describe it, together with the interior distress that it provokes, ancient monastic literature borrowed from the then current translations of the Bible an expression which in those days still possessed the supple vigour of the image that had inspired it: "*diatribè tès kardias*"; in latin: "*contritio cordis*" (contrition of heart) or "*contritio mentis*" (contrition of mind). It is found in all the languages through which the most ancient witnesses of the monastic experience have reached us, which proves the capital importance that was attributed to it. Under Cassian's pen, it is frequently joined to the word "humility", of which it is practically a synonym, and to which it gives concrete relief: "*contritis et humiliatis cordibus*" (with humble and contrite hearts). It would be good to retain if possible the rough and unrefined meaning of the original, which was unfortunately lost by most of our modern languages. We are not speaking here of course of "contrition", as modern spiritual literature understands it, but rather of a heart that has been really broken, crushed, reduced to pieces.

Among other ancient texts, we remember the moving description of the harrying of the soul by temptations, which was left us in an Egyptian document attributed to Saint Makarius the Great, and known as *Letter to his sons*. We see the temptations come one after the other, every one more humiliating than the last, and every time the monk narrowly misses a fall, when grace - a strength of the Holy Spirit, says Saint Makarius - intervenes to save him at the very last moment. Why so many hard crises? Because God wants to teach him, explains Makarius, "that this is what makes him strong. The brother monk now really knows how to give glory to God in all humility and broken-heartedness, as David says: 'The sacrifice acceptable to God is a broken spirit' (*Psalm* 50:17). For it is from this hard battle that humility and brokenness of heart, kindness and gentleness are born."

Such descriptions of the deep distress felt in times of temptation, abound in the monastic tradition. They help to dismiss from our minds the myth of the "ascetic-champion monk", that became popular in the romantic historiography of the 1900s. In times of temptation, the monk, and every Christian, is nothing more than a poor servant of Yahweh, reduced to a boundless trust in grace. "Believe me, my brother", said Isaac the Syrian, "you have not yet understood the strength of temptation or the subtlety of its tricks". But one day, experience will teach you, and "you will find yourself before it like a panicking child. All your knowledge will be turned to confusion, like that of a little child. And your spirit which seemed so firmly established in God, your precise knowledge, your well-balanced thought, are all immersed in an ocean of doubt. One thing only can help you to overcome: humility. As soon as you seize hold of it, all of temptation's power dissolves."

Co-operating with God's painful teaching necessarily means to accept going in the same direction as it does, not fleeing before the humiliation inflicted by temptation, but, somehow, becoming wedded to it. This is done, not out of some unconscious form of masochism, but because we feel in it the secret source of the only true life. In biblical terms, we would say: because that is where the heart of stone will be broken, and where the heart of flesh will appear, temporarily hidden behind so many unconscious defences. Indeed, this breaking up constitutes a redoubtable trial for a person's psychological make-up. The narcissist who looks at himself in the mirror will here literally break into pieces. The Pharisee hidden in our hearts, rebels against such a dethronement for he will no longer be able to save appearances. And yet, ancient authors insist that we must really go as far as this, because it is in humiliations which have been accepted, and I would say spiritually "digested", that salvation awaits us. As this saying advises: "When we are tempted, let us abase ourselves lower, for then God who sees our weakness protects us. But if we lift ourselves up, he withdraws his protection and we perish". "Submit to the grace of God in a spirit of poverty for fear that, drawn by the spirit of pride, you should lose the fruit of your work".

Such then is the part of man, according to the Fathers, in the painful confrontation between, on the one hand, a freedom wounded by sin, and on the other, restoring grace which reigns supreme but which is respectful of our freedom. This part is an indispensable condition for true humility, and ensures that any other virtue we have does not become a form of self-deceit, reflected advantageously by our narcissistic self-mirror, or warmly applauded by our virtuous super-ego. Even chastity itself is in fact such a gift of God that it is possible, thinks Cassian, only for those who know how to welcome it in a totally broken heart. The role of man, tossed between his freedom and grace, is the peaceful acceptance of a broken heart. It is the role of an emptying which must take place before we can receive, and all the more confidently aspire to grace.

If there is an effort to be made on our part, it is that of facing up to our human fragility, perpetually confronted with its own limits. Cassian salutes it, with some emphasis, as an endless humiliation. We are here at the heart of the Gospel, at the critical point of all asceticism and of every Christian mysticism. According to Pseudo-Makarius "having our hearts totally broken" is the foundation of the Christian faith.

V. Christian Asceticism

*T*he temptations mentioned above are those that God chooses for us, and doubtless are what is best for us, but there are also the ones that one chooses for oneself. As I mentioned earlier, the monk in particular seems to go out to meet temptation head on by embracing a style of life where asceticism occupies an important place. Is it because he is stronger than others? That would really be the supreme illusion. If the monk chooses a life of asceticism, it is, because he must discover with his own eyes that he is the weakest of all. For an authentically Christian asceticism enjoys the same status as temptation and must give rise to the same process, which will produce the same fruits, humility and love, "*humilis caritas*", humble love. Without this, it would be a perfectly pagan work, in which Aristotle and Cicero might recognise themselves, but not Jesus on Easter morning. As Isaac the Syrian reminds us: "As long as someone is not humble, he will get no reward for his asceticism. Reward is not given because of asceticism, but because of humility... Reward is not given for virtue either, but for the humility that is born of both. But if humility is not present, asceticism and virtue are in vain".

Far from being punishments, temptations and trials are the only way by which God will one day make us fit for his fullness. Indeed, thinks Isaac the Syrian, God continuously keeps in reserve "relaxations and consolations without number", which he wants to flood us with, but our lack of disposition obliges him to send us "affliction instead of relaxation, amendment instead of help". But if humility had been installed within us, there would have been no need to prepare such a difficult education. Moreover God is obliged to continue as soon as he notices that a first humiliation was not enough, and that pride is turning to its own profit the first fruits of holiness. About this the same Isaac writes: "As soon as grace notices a little bit of self-satisfaction slipping into someone who starts to have a good opinion of himself, it immediately allows temptations to strengthen and even to have the upper hand, until this man learns to know his weakness and to flee in order to cling humbly to God. For in this way we acquire the stature of a perfect man, in faith in the Son of God, and we are raised up to love".

But temptation is not the only school of humility, for sin itself, allowed by God when there is no other way, may become a way to salvation. We have only to think of King David from whom, in Psalm 50, spiritual tradition borrowed the image of a "humble and contrite heart". David had indeed fallen into serious sin, but his sin became a *felix culpa*, a happy fault, which put him on the way to salvation.

In an entire sermon on humility, Saint Basil recalls the fall of the Apostle Peter. He loved Jesus more than others, but had flattered himself too much for it. God "therefore gave him up to his own human cowardice and he fell into disowning the Lord, but his fall made him wiser and taught him to keep on his guard. He learned to spare the weak, having learned his own weakness. He now knew clearly that it was by the strength of Christ that he had been protected when he was in danger of perishing for his lack of faith. In the storm he had been saved by the hand of Christ when he was at the point of sinking in the waters". The author concludes a little later: "Humility often liberates the one who has sinned often and heavily". That is why Saint Isaac of

Niniveh did not hesitate to call the monk's failures the "guards" of his justice. "God allows these failures", he wrote, "so that faults and transgressions may become an occasion of humility. Humility protects the ascetic works of the greatest, not only by preventing them from pride, but by humiliating them by the recall of their faults. Thus they will receive an even greater reward". For even God's most excellent gifts, unaccompanied by temptation, "are a disaster for those who receive them... If God grants you some gift, persuade him to teach you also how this gift can help you make progress in humility... Or beg him to take it away, so that it doesn't become the cause of your downfall. For not everyone is capable of being fulfilled without damaging himself".

If temptation should end with a fall, it is not therefore because of a lack of generosity, but rather of humility. And if the sinner knows how to watch for grace, which never ceases working within him, as it were from behind the sin, then the opportunity provided by sin could well be that at last he finds the narrow gate - and especially the low, the very low door - which alone opens on to the Kingdom. "Above all we must not despair of not being as we should be", advises Saint Peter of Damascus. "Of course, your sin is evil, but if you say: 'That sin is my own condemnation, but even more so, it is God's own mercy', then you repent and he receives your repentance like that of the prodigal son... The one who sins, but does not despair, puts himself lower than all other creatures. He does not dare to blame or condemn anyone. Rather, he admires God's love for man, he gives thanks to his benefactor. If he does not follow the devil who, having submitted him to sin, now urges him on to despair, then his part is with God. Within him he possesses thanksgiving, patience, fear of God..., he does not judge so as not to be judged". For it is possible for the worst temptation not to be that which preceded sin, but that which followed it: the temptation to despair, from which, once more, humility which has now been learned at last, will allow us to escape.

In the end the feeling that will predominate in the humble man is an unshakeable confidence in God's mercy, of which he has had some intimation even through his falls. How could he still doubt? Again Isaac the Syrian paints us a picture, which is very near to our own daily experience. In a text taken from his recently discovered works he says: "Will God forgive me those things that pain me and whose memory torment me? Things towards which, even if they horrify me, I let myself slide again and again? And when they have been committed, the suffering they cause me is greater than the sting of a scorpion. I abhor them, and I find myself always among them, and when I have painfully repented, I return to them all the same, unhappy man that I am". This, adds Isaac, "is what many people who fear God think, though they aspire to virtue and regret their sins, while their weakness obliges them to take notice of the falls that it causes: they spend their time caught between sin and repentance". However, adds Isaac again, "do not doubt your salvation... His mercy is much greater than you might think, his grace, more far-reaching than you dare ask. He ceaselessly watches for the least spark of regret in someone who has let himself be robbed of a portion of justice in his battle with passions and with sin".

For this divine game of temptation and of grace is a game of love. Far from being an executioner, God reveals himself to be an infinitely loving and patient teacher, gentle and humble in heart, who shapes us in his own image. Saint John Cassian has sketched for us the most moving picture. In the history of our temptations, he sees the expression of God's incomparable delicacy, and he dares to compare it to the tender game which takes place between a mother and her little child, with the object of accelerating his development towards adulthood: "For a long time she carries her child in her arms", writes Cassian, "until at last she teaches him how to walk. First, she lets him crawl. Then, she sets him on his feet, holds him by her right hand, to teach him to place one foot in front of the other. Soon, she lets go of his hand for a moment; but should she see him stagger, she quickly takes it up again, supporting his hesitating steps. She lifts him up if he has fallen, or retains him at the point of falling, or, on the contrary, lets him fall gently, only to lift him up again..." It is in this way, concludes Cassian, that the heavenly Father acts with each one of us. He knows more than us "who he must carry on the lap of his grace, who he must bring to trial under his eyes... while letting him be master of his freedom, helping him in his work, answering him when he calls, not abandoning him when he seeks, and sometimes withdrawing him unawares from danger". More than anywhere else, it is at the hour of temptation that we find ourselves "in the lap of grace".

The humility that will thus be born cannot be reduced to greater or lesser self-esteem, more or less temperance. It is something of another order altogether, for it transcends the domain of qualities and virtues; it can be identified with the new being, born from grace by baptism, and bearing at last all his fruit. Should we still want to speak about virtue, it would be an all-encompassing virtue, a heart of stone crushed and resurrected into a heart of flesh, from which all other virtues spring. As once again Isaac the Syrian said: "Humility is God's clothing".

Such a man knows himself to be weak and a sinner, but he finally turned his eyes away from his own misery and looked only upon God's mercy. The breaking of his heart, his contrition, has gradually been transformed into a humble and peaceful joy, into love and thanksgiving. No fault, no sin is denied or excused, but they have been drowned and engulfed by mercy. "Where sin increased, grace abounded all the more" (*Romans* 5:20). Everything that had been broken by sin is restored by grace into something better, much better, than before. His prayer still bears the traces of his sin and of his misery, and perhaps always will, but from now on his fault is a happy fault, a *felix culpa*, as we sing at every Easter Vigil, a guilt that is engulfed by love. Between contrition and thanksgiving, there is now almost no difference. Both meld together, and the tears of repentance become also tears of love.

Little by little this joyful sentiment of contrition comes to predominate our spiritual experience. In this asceticism of poverty - *patientia pauperum* - a new man rises every day. He is all peace, joy, benevolence, gentleness. He remains forever marked by repentance, but it is a repentance full of joy and love which rises up anew everywhere and always, and remains as the backdrop of his search for God. Henceforth such a man has reached a profound peace, for he has been broken and reconstructed in his entire being by pure grace. He barely recognises himself. He has become different. He has closely touched sin's deep abyss, but at the same moment he was thrown into the abyss of mercy. He has at last learned to lay down his arms before God, to stop defending himself from him. He has renounced any personal justice and has no more ambitions of holiness. His hands are empty, or keep nothing more than his misery, but he dares to expose them to mercy. God has at last become God for him. And nothing but God, which means *Salvator*, that is, Saviour from sin. He is even almost reconciled to his own sin, as God has become reconciled with him. He is happy and grateful to be weak. He no longer seeks his own perfection: "We have all become like one who is unclean, and all our righteous deeds are like a polluted garment" (*Isaiah* 64:6). He possesses his own justice in God alone. Only his wounds remain, but tended and healed by mercy and blossoming into marvels. He only knows how to give thanks and praise to God, who is always at work in him to accomplish his marvels.

To his brethren and his loved ones, he has become a kindly and gentle friend. He understands their weaknesses. He no longer has any confidence in himself, but rather in God alone. His whole life is taken up with the all-powerful love of God. That is why he is also poor, really poor - a poor man in spirit - and near to the poor and every form of poverty, whether spiritual or corporal. He thinks he is the first among all sinners, but a pardoned sinner. That is why he knows how to relate as an equal and a brother with all the sinners in the world. He feels near to them, because he does not feel he is better than others. His favourite prayer is that of the publican, which has become like his own breathing, like the beatings of the heart of the world, his deepest desire is for salvation and healing: "Lord Jesus, have pity on me a sinner!"

And there remains in him a single desire: that God should once again put him to the test, so that he may once again discover his proximity; once again embrace humble patience and trust him boundlessly with even greater love. This patience and humility make him like Jesus and allow God to renew his marvels in him.

When I started this work, I wished to mention certain philosophers, pagan and Christian, in order to call into question their capacity to understand evangelical humility only by the light of natural reason. I would like to finish by quoting another philosopher, a Christian one: Jean Guitton. In his last work, written when he was almost one hundred years old, and a few months before his recent death, he handed over what he called his *Philosophical Testament*. In a text whose wit is only equalled by his humour and perhaps also his irony, he sees himself on his death-bed, receiving a last visit from all the great people he had known physically or spiritually on this earth. And so various famous people file past: Pascal, Bergson, Paul VI whose friend he was, El Greco, Leopold Senghor, General De Gaulle whom he followed fervently, Socrates, Maurice Blondel, Dante, even François Miterrand, who, somewhat surprisingly, trusted him. All these personages come to prepare him for the Judgement that he is soon to undergo, as his death is imminent. But his cause is not secure in advance. He is conscious of all the traps he came near to fall into during his life as a philosopher, of which the greatest, he confesses, were arrogance and vainglory. He is however, saved *in extremis*, partly by the pleading of Saint Thérèse of the Child Jesus, partly by the last words that the Judge allows him to speak before deliberations on his fate begin. Let us listen to these words that Guitton borrowed from one of the greatest mystics of all time: "Jesus then asked me: 'Jean, do you have anything else to add?' I answered: 'I stand before you, Jesus, my Creator, my Saviour and my Judge'. While saying these words, I tried to take a paper out of my pocket, I finally succeeded and unfolded it, but I was too moved and the paper fell to the ground... Thérèse jumped up... She picked up the paper. I was very tired. I told Thérèse in a neutral voice: 'Read it yourself. It is from the admirable Ruysbroek. That is how I would have wished to live and to die'. So then Thérèse read the following:

"When with eyes that are burning with love, a man considers within himself the immensity of God... when he then looks at himself, counts his attempts against this immense and faithful Lord... he does not know a contempt deep enough to satisfy him... He falls into a strange astonishment, the astonishment of not being able to despise himself deeply enough... He resigns himself then to the will of God..., and, with an intimate abnegation, he finds true peace..., that nothing can disturb... Our very sins have become for us sources of humility and love... To be plunged into humility is to be plunged into God, for God is the bottom of the abyss... Humility obtains things that are too high to be taught; it reaches and possesses what speech does not reach."

Biographies

St John Climacus

Born *circa* 525 in Syria, died 606 Mount Sinai. Withdrew from the world at a young age to join the monks that lived in the region of Mount Sinai. He lived as a hermit for most of his life except for a brief spell as the abbot of the Sinai monks. He was well known for his wisdom and learning and became especially famous for his book '*Ladder of Perfection*'.

St Anthony of Egypt

Born in Egypt 251, died 356. Born to a rich Christian family, when he inherited his parents' wealth he sold everything and gave the money to the poor. He then went into the desert to live a solitary life of harsh asceticism, eating only bread and water all his life. His attempts at solitude were constantly disturbed as his fame and reputation for holiness grew. He eventually founded two monasteries and became known as the father of monasticism.

St John Cassian

Born 360 in Provence, died 435 in Marseilles. Travelled from Southern Gaul with the desire of finding a way of life that would bring him to sanctity. He stayed with the monks of the desert in Egypt and the Holy Land and went on to Constantinople to become a favourite disciple of St John Chrysostom. He returned to Marseilles and founded two monasteries, one for men the other for women. Responsible for bringing Eastern Monasticism to the West.

St Makarius the Great

Born *circa* 300 in Upper Egypt, died 390. Was a pioneering hermit and disciple of Saint Anthony of Egypt. Founder of a monastic community in the Scetic desert. Ordained at the age of 40. His sanctity drew many followers, and his desert community numbered thousands at his death. Fought the Aryan heresy.

Isaac the Syrian

Born in Kurdistan, died *circa* 700 in Northern Iraq. Briefly bishop of Nineveh of the heretical Nestorian Church, but began and ended his adult life as a monk. His writings were considered too Catholic for his Nestorian peers.

St Peter of Damascus

Died 750 in Damascus. The bishop of Damascus, Syria, at the time of the Islamic conquest of the region. He was seized by the Muslims for preaching against Muhammad and condemned to death. His captors tortured, blinded, crucified, and finally beheaded him.

Rediscovering Virtue

In a world where it has become normal for individuals to decide for themselves what is right and what is wrong, the traditional Christian virtues are not often mentioned. However, now more than ever, the sure moral compass provided by justice, religion, prudence, temperance and courage is necessary to live a truly Christian life in faith hope and love.

The *Deeper Christianity Series* delves into the mysteries of Christianity, opening up the spiritual treasures of the Church.

Fr Bernard Green S.D.S. has been a Seminary and College Lecturer and pastor on the White Mountain Apache Reservation in Arizona. He is currently Director of the Institute for the Study of Catholic Faith and Life in Tempe, Arizona.

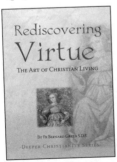

ISBN: 978 1 86082 454 8

CTS Code: SP 20

8 Deadly Sins

The Church has settled on a list of 7 mortal sins but the Fathers of the Church more often referred to 8. The deadly or capital sins - covetousness, envy, sloth, gluttony, lust, anger, vainglory and pride - are the most significant and insidious temptations with which we must contend. A first step in countering their influence is understanding their psychological and spiritual roots in human experience. Standing humbly in the truth about ourselves, we will appreciate the power of God's love to heal and strengthen our nature, for love is not jealous or boastful, not arrogant or rude, not irritable or resentful.

The *Deeper Christianity Series* delves into the mysteries of Christianity, opening up the spiritual treasures of the Church.

Vivian Boland, OP is Master of Students for the English Dominicans, lectures in theology at St Mary's, Twickenham and Blackfriars, Oxford. He also preaches retreats, and writes on theology and spirituality.

ISBN: 978 1 86082 460 9

CTS Code: SP 21

8 Deadly Sins

LEARNING TO DEFEND THE LIFE OF GRACE

BY VIVIAN BOLAND, OP

DEEPER CHRISTIANITY SERIES

The Little Way
of St Thérèse of Lisieux

Hardly twenty-four years of age, Thérèse Martin died of tuberculosis in Normandy in 1897. From a large family, her mother had died of breast cancer when Thérèse was only four. Her father, a master watchmaker, died after years in a mental hospital. These writings show how it is that this young French woman, in such a short life, has inspired millions. In recognition of her special teaching mission for God's people, the Church has proclaimed her a Doctor of the Church - the only woman apart from St Catherine of Sienna and St Teresa of Avila.

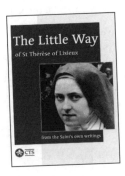

ISBN: 978 1 86082 389 7

CTS Code: D 306

A Rule of Life

How can we encourage our Christian life to grow and mature into holiness? Our wills are often weak, the environment hostile, and we can be so busy. This is where a personal Rule of Life can be invaluable, to help us live our lives in regular contact with God, each day, week, month and season, and so to love and serve Our Lord and our neighbour. We need to acquire good habits to live out a Christian life, and this booklet, drawing deeply on the experience of Christians over the ages, helps us to map out the basic elements.

Fr Michael Woodgate is a priest of the Southwark Diocese and teaches at Wonersh seminary.

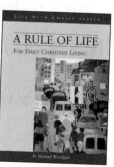

ISBN: 978 1 86082 440 1

CTS Code: Do 759